#SUCCESSFUL CORPORATE LEARNING **tweet**
Book05
Everything You Need to Know about Knowledge Management
in Practice in 140 Characters or Less

By Michael Prevou and Mitchell Levy

Foreword by Kent Greenes

E-mail: info@thinkaha.com
20660 Stevens Creek Blvd., Suite 210
Cupertino, CA 95014

Published by THiNKaha®, a Happy About® imprint
20660 Stevens Creek Blvd., Suite 210, Cupertino, CA 95014
http://thinkaha.com

First Printing: August 2012
Paperback ISBN: 978-1-61699-088-6 (1-61699-088-0)
eBook ISBN: 978-1-61699-089-3 (1-61699-089-9)
Place of Publication: Silicon Valley, California, USA
Paperback Library of Congress Number: 2012932532

Advance Praise

"What fun! Mike and Mitchell have crowdsourced a book on KM. You get a firsthand look at what your peers think about KM topics like strategy, metrics, and leadership. And you get practical experience from one of the people who made KM really work in the U.S. Army."
Nancy M. Dixon, Author, *Common Knowledge: How Companies Thrive by Sharing What They Know,* **Co-author,** *CompanyCommand: Unleashing the Power of the Army Profession*

"A must-read for all professionals involved in managing, sharing, and creating knowledge in their organization!"
Eileen U. Godinez, DM, Faculty, Grantham University

"Brilliant design, captures the essence of learning quickly in context necessary to keep pace in our globally connected world."
Bradley C. Hilton, Co-author, "Knowledge-Enabled High-Performing Teams of Leaders" in *Knowledge Management Handbook: Collaboration and Social Networking* **(2nd edition)**

"If you want the big picture of knowledge management in a clear, simple format, this is THE book. It covers the seven essentials of a world-class KM program. And with the authors' experience, you get precise advice on what to do and what to avoid in implementing KM in your real world situation. You can't do better than to start here."
Bruce Jeffrey, Co-author, *On the Same Page: How to Engage Employees and Accelerate Growth*

"Michael Prevou and Mitchell Levy created a great practical and concise overview of what counts when dealing with knowledge flows. The innovative format blending summaries with expert quotes provides you with the essence of learning on the topic."
Frank Leistner, Chief Knowledge Officer, Global Professional Services, SAS, Author, *Mastering Organizational Knowledge Flow: How to Make Knowledge Sharing Work*

Dedication

To the men and women of the Armed Forces whom I have worked with on KM projects for these past six years. Remember, your tour of duty is not over until you have shared what you have learned.

And to my daughters who are finding their way in the world—may your lives be nothing less than phenomenal.

Mike Prevou

Acknowledgments

To my wife, Sheila, and my business partner, Holly, for giving me time to write.

To the many KM practitioners who contributed tweets and mentored me through my learning journey:

Holly Baxter	Mike Hower	Rick Morris
Christie Beverly	Dorothy Leonard	Chris Nail
Nancy Dixon	Chip Levine	John Nelson
Steffen Doberstein	Frank Leistner	Patrick Sullivan
Eileen Godinez	Jay Liebowitz	Eric Trujillo
Kent Greenes	Mike Kitchens	Mark Uhart
Brad Hilton	Linda McGurn	Denny Zimmerman

To Mitchell (*@HappyAbout*) and his team for keeping me on track.

To my team at Strategic Knowledge Solutions for their ideas and support.

Mike Prevou

Why We Wrote This Book

Knowledge creates the capacity for effective action. It is a key component for any organization, especially one striving to become a learning organization. Today, the increasing complexity of both the corporate environment and organizations' internal workings, combined with the speed and volume of information, the pressure for innovation and adaptability, and the scarcity of attention, makes managing knowledge central to an organization's success. Knowledge management (KM) is the deliberate approach to applying knowledge to gain or maintain a competitive edge. KM is an essential business strategy and must be aligned with business objectives that are designed to improve performance and outcomes. KM is also crucial to winning the learning competition required to bring ideas and products to market faster.

We wanted to write this book for two reasons. First, because the concept *knowledge management* is surrounded by much confusion and baggage. Too often it is thought of as a technology or tool. Rather, it is a holistic approach integrating key components in the right balance to create an effective environment for knowledge to be identified, captured, shared, and applied to some advantage. We want to help clarify what KM *is* and what it *is not* so leaders and managers have a better understanding of how KM can help their organizations learn, share, collaborate, and perform.

Second, we wanted to provide a simple and practical outline for how we design and communicate a KM strategy and talk about how that strategy must be aligned with business goals and objectives. Organizations should not be practicing KM just for the sake of practicing KM. Without a strategy to guide their actions, we see organizations jumping from one initiative to another or one technology tool to another with no apparent methodology or link to their corporate goals and objectives.

KM should be a deliberate and continuous strategy to get the right knowledge to the right people at the right time, helping people share what they know and put it into action in ways that improve individual and organizational performance. KM is a young discipline and is suffering growing pains as different camps attempt to define it in their own terms. To validate our rethinking of KM, we used a number of blogs and communities of practice to gain input and feedback for each section. KM practitioners in the public, private, and non-profit sectors provided practical, on-the-ground advice that will help corporate leaders understand what KM is, why they need it, how it aligns with and accomplishes their business objectives, and how to design, measure, and implement a KM program.

In the appendices, we have provided an outline of a sample KM strategy and a set of KM principles. KM practitioners and organizational leaders can use these to guide the conversation about managing the Knowledge Environment™ and improving knowledge flow. Effective KM is as much art as it is science; it requires attention be given to a number of core components to create an ecosystem that enables knowledge to flow into and through an organization. Our hope is that you will share these "ahas" and provide us your thoughts and stories about KM in your organization.

Mike Prevou

Twitter: *@mikeprevou*
mike@strategicKS.com

Mitchell Levy

Twitter: *@HappyAbout*
mitchell.levy@happyabout.info

How to Read a THiNKaha® Book
A Note from the Publisher

The THiNKaha series is the CliffsNotes of the 21st century. The value of these books is that they are contextual in nature. Although the actual words won't change, their meaning will change every time you read one as your context will change. Here's how to read one of these books and have it work for you.

1. Read a THiNKaha book (these slim and handy books should only take approximately 15–20 minutes of your time!) and write down one to three "aha" moments you had while reading it.

    > "Aha" moments are looked at as "actionable" moments—think of a specific project you're working on, an event, a sales deal, a personal issue, etc. and see how the ahas in this book can inspire your own "aha!" moment, something that you can specifically act on.

2. Mark your calendar to re-read this book again in 30 days.

3. Repeat step #1 and write down one to three "aha" moments that grab you this time. I guarantee that they will be different than the first time.

After reading a THiNKaha book, writing down your "aha" moments, re-reading it, and writing down more "aha" moments, you'll begin to see how these books contextually apply to you. THiNKaha books advocate for continuous, life-long learning. They will help you transform your "aha" moments into actionable items with tangible results until you no longer have to say "aha!" to these moments—they'll become part of your daily practice as you continue to grow and learn.

As CEO of THiNKaha, I definitely practice what I preach. I read #CORPORATE CULTURE tweet, #LEADERSHIP tweet, and #TEAMWORK tweet once a month and take away two to three different action items from each of them every time. Please e-mail me your "aha" moments.

Mitchell Levy, CEO
publisher@thinkaha.com

Contents

Foreword by Kent Greenes

The rapid rate of change and increased complexity of business has outpaced our abilities to learn and perform as organizations, teams, and individuals. When these factors are combined with the emergence of competition from sources never before imaginable, we can no longer afford to rely on traditional knowledge sharing and transfer methods. Knowledge management (KM) is one of the most powerful new enablers in a business leader's toolkit.

Social media, microblogging, advanced search engines, and new collaboration software (such as SharePoint) are making a difference in knowledge sharing and transfer because of three new realities in the marketplace: the need for speed, complex problems with no right answers, and too much information.

The need for speed. No matter what, knowledge collaboration, sharing, and transfer have to be fast. In today's marketplace, speed is everything. Speed is so critical now that people are searching for expertise and content in a limited amount of time.

We need to learn at the speed of work to solve new problems quicker, accelerate innovation, get our products and services to market faster, and outperform the competition. Learning from experience is the source of most of the knowledge we need to perform. Everyone from the boardroom to the field agrees that learning before doing a task or project is how experience becomes explicit and moveable. But it takes too much time, so it doesn't get done. When we weave the tools into our business processes and organizational structures to share and find nuggets of bite-sized, quickly digestible knowledge, we reduce the time it takes to learn before doing and to disseminate learning after doing, which means people will actually use the knowledge!

No right answers. Tasks and decisions that could be effectively handled by an individual in earlier times now exceed the scope of a single person.

This new workplace reality is driving a fundamental shift in learning and knowledge transfer from the traditional "one-to-many" approach to a "many-to-many" way of learning. This approach informs thinking and generates new ideas and solutions. KM enables many people to share their knowledge with many others and brings the wisdom of the crowds to solving big organizational problems much faster than before. It's an awesome capability for leveraging cognitive diversity to help inform our thinking.

But that's not all KM does. It also makes knowledge sharing and transfer more effective. It puts information in context, helps connect us with expertise, and provides us a deliberate way to capture and transfer experience before it retires and departs the organization. It helps us identify best business practices and the conditions that make them relevant and helps us organize the volumes of content we have available as a usable resource. Done right, KM forces us to be organized, thoughtful, and concise in what we share. This is what our brains really like and need—knowledge in short, sharp chunks.

Drowning in information but never enough knowledge. Let's face it, there's just too much data and information out there, but I have never heard anyone say they had too much knowledge. And information sources are multiplying at an ever-increasing rate. This is a great thing if we can manage the environment. But it also makes it difficult and time-consuming to find the right knowledge you need when you need it. By the nature of how it works, KM can provide a channel of relevancy to help ease the weight of too much information.

And finally, we share with people we know and trust. This means each connection carries some context to help us make sense of what is being shared. This automatically reduces the herculean task we face sorting and sifting through the vast amount of knowledge available. It's no wonder people these days are searching for an answer to the question of how to manage knowledge more effectively.

Michael and Mitchell have done a great thing here. They have combined their experience in KM and learning to give us nuggets of insights from real practitioners that we can quickly tap and digest to inform our thinking. Their focus on the Knowledge Environment™ is right on target. Their orientation on people and processes versus technology is a breath of fresh air. It's now up to us to use this wealth of advice to learn before, during, and after and optimize our knowledge management efforts.

Kent Greenes

Founder of Greenes Consulting and previous Head of Knowledge Management for British Petroleum and Science Applications International Corporation

Knowledge is the capacity to act.

—*Karl-Erik Sveiby*

Knowledge is information that changes something or somebody—either by becoming grounds for actions or by making an individual (or organization) capable of different or more effective action.

—*Peter Drucker in* The New Realities (1989)

We are drowning in information, but starving for knowledge.

—*Anonymous*

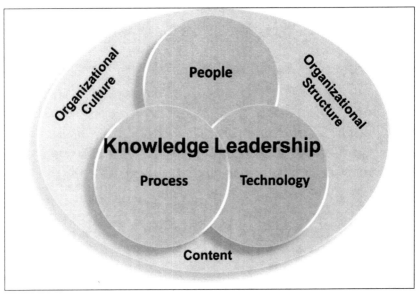

The Knowledge Environment™

Section I
What Is Knowledge Management?

KM is a deliberate approach to help organizations effectively use and reuse what they know (both tacit and explicit) to achieve a sustained competitive advantage.

Knowledge exists in the heads of people. In a business context, it is "what our employees know about their customers, one another, products, processes, mistakes, and successes, whether that knowledge is tacit or explicit" (O'Dell and Hubert 2011). It is our ability to access, learn from, and use this knowledge for a competitive advantage that drives the need for us to manage knowledge in our organizations.

While knowledge management (KM) is a relatively new discipline, it is often misunderstood and hard to quantify in terms of results. One of the reasons it is so misunderstood is the difficulty in visualizing and communicating how people manage knowledge. Our default frame of reference causes us to focus on managing documents, artifacts, and the technology systems used to store and collect these artifacts, rather than on the full spectrum of both tacit and explicit knowledge linked to improving business objectives and creating results. If we can reframe our thinking to one that manages the environment in which we want knowledge to flow, then we can address the components of that environment as tangible items that we can design, build, measure, and manage.

While the three elements of people, processes, and technology have formed the foundation for KM in the past, they are no longer sufficient to outline an effective knowledge environment. KM must orient on at least seven components we call the Knowledge Environment™ (Prevou 2011) so we can reduce the barriers and improve the way in which knowledge moves through the organization. The Knowledge Environment™ consists of: people, processes, technology, organizational structure, content, organizational culture, and knowledge leadership. Each component must be addressed and integrated in the right balance for an effective KM effort. Likewise, KM must also be linked to the goals and objectives of the organization and focused on closing performance gaps.

Managing what we know and who knows it is too important to our success for it to be left to happenstance. KM must put people first and serve as a deliberate approach to help effectively use and reuse what we know to achieve a sustained competitive advantage. This holistic strategy to manage the entire Knowledge Environment™ is a must for any modern-day organization.

1

KM is about sharing tacit and explicit knowledge, breaking down silos, and connecting the workforce to improve performance.

2

KM is a way of conducting everyday business to ensure our corporate knowledge is embedded in our business processes.

3

KM is socially driven, linking people across the organizational boundaries to share what they know.

4

KM is about managing professional conversation by using social applications that link people to people and people to content.

5

KM is required for organizations to work across organizational boundaries and to improve workflow, ideation, learning, and performance.

6

KM is about finding experts, connecting people, and solving problems in a more effective way.

7

KM is critical if we are to improve the rate at which we learn, develop expertise, and build cross-boundary teams.

8

KM must be aligned with the company performance goals and objectives. It helps us do our jobs better, to improve our capacity to act.

9

KM is a means for managing information overload, change, and continuous innovation.

10

KM is about creating knowledge flow and enabling the disciplined management of all the components of the Knowledge Environment™.

11

KM is about reducing costs using our existing knowledge and increasing revenues by creating new knowledge.

12

KM is about making connections between those who know and those who need to know (know-what/who, know-how, know-why).

13

KM is about changing the company culture from "Knowledge Is Power" to "Knowledge Shared Is Power."

14

KM connects the art of leadership and intuition to the science of management and control.

15

KM is about understanding how knowledge is developed and shared in a company.

16

KM is necessary to ensure knowledge is moving through the organization and the means to measure it are in place.

17

KM provides a disciplined approach and a set of tools to what would otherwise be happenstance.

18

KM is a holistic approach that covers everything from creating new knowledge to managing documents and records.

19

KM is about retaining knowledge as people transition and retire and using that knowledge to develop the next generation of leaders.

20

KM is connecting people to share what they know.

21

KM is focused on moving actionable knowledge from people to people, not storing information and data in large repositories.

22

KM is the effort undertaken to understand what an organization knows and what it does not know, and how to close that gap.

23

KM involves an analysis of business processes to improve the efficiency and effectiveness of business functions, activities, and tasks.

24

KM can help instill discipline within an organization's workflow and business processes.

25

KM enables the creation, organization, maintenance, and transfer of knowledge.

26

KM is the way that Gen X and Y workers are accustomed to collaborating and working.

27

KM is about aligning processes and people to create a culture of collaboration.

28

KM provides the ways and means to achieve business goals and objectives by leveraging what we know to work smarter.

Section II
What Knowledge Management Is Not

Oftentimes, when people are discussing knowledge management, the conversation quickly turns to things that KM is not—like the technical details of data storage solutions or the latest collaborative tools—rather than staying focused on the goals that KM can accomplish (i.e., business drivers such as improving human performance or business processes, or the creation of a capability to find and connect expertise with those who need it). As noted by many of the practitioners who contributed content to this book, technology alone cannot share knowledge or make the complex decisions for us. It can store data and information and prod us to action, but ultimately, it is only a tool that must be integrated into our work environment and applied in context.

Successful KM is more about connecting people to people and people to content than anything else. Technology is a key enabler, especially today when we need to span time and geographical boundaries to connect a global workforce. But technology is only an enabler, a tool. Understanding and considering each of the seven components of the Knowledge Environment™ and creating the proper balance, like in any ecosystem, is paramount to effective KM.

When considering a knowledge flow problem or gap, first ask, "What are we trying to accomplish and why?" without any discussion of technology. Then, and only then, discuss how technology can enhance and enable that process. KM should be used to solve business problems and should not be an end unto itself.

29

KM is not technology driven. Technology is an enabler—it cannot share or make decisions for us.

30

KM *enables* business processes—it's not a separate or additional business function, an extra duty, or a step in a process.

31

Remember, knowledge must move to be valuable. Do your KM systems move it, or just store it?

32

KM is not run or managed by the IT team. They simply enable it like a plumber enables the flow of drinking water.

33

KM is not narrowly focused on mining the knowledge contained in documents. More than 80% of corporate knowledge is in people's heads!

34

It's everyone's duty to understand how KM fits into the company processes. Don't designate KM to one position or team.

35

Don't assume people will access and use the information that is dumped into large repositories or databases.

36

Use KM to enable knowledge flow. It's not about organizational knowledge control, seniority, or position. It's about flow.

37

KM is not about static content or static websites. It is dynamic; it enables business decisions.

38

KM is not an independent operation. It does not create value on its own; it must be linked to solving real business problems.

39

KM is not discovering new information but understanding information in a new way, enabling us to think and act with insight and wisdom.

40

KM is not about applying a technology solution for storing and passing information.

41

KM is not about working alone. It is about connecting with people and relevant content, and contributing in a meaningful way.

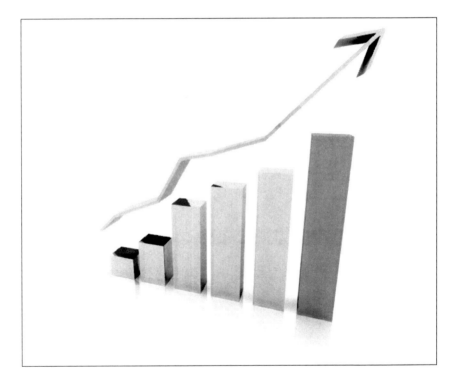

Section III
Benefits of a Knowledge Management Program

The benefits of a KM program could include improved performance; increased productivity and profits; improved innovation; better, faster decisions; cost savings; reduced loss of knowledge and expertise from retiring and transitioning workers; happier workers; and increased individual/team efficiency and effectiveness. If your KM program is aligned directly with your business strategy (as we recommend), you are practicing KM for the benefit of your organization's bottom line. Your organization's KM and information technology practitioners and managers should be able to directly link almost every KM and IT activity to a business goal and objective.

According to the Economist Intelligence Study "Foresight 2020," KM is one of the five key trends that will determine competitiveness in this decade. For businesses to compete successfully, they will need access to actionable information and expertise faster and with more context and relevance than ever before. With so much riding on our need to connect our workforce and share what we know to learn from one another and produce for our organizations, KM cannot be left to happenstance. The benefits and rewards will be commensurate with an effective program that manages the entire spectrum of the Knowledge Environment™.

42

KM helps you learn faster and more effectively than your competition.

43

KM helps you manage the increasing volume and speed of big data and the requirement to constantly innovate and grow.

44

KM creates faster, more informed decision making, shorter time-to-market cycle, and improved employee and customer satisfaction.

45

KM improves return on investment, efficiency of processes, and information technology.

46

KM helps us connect the workforce across time, space, and organizational boundaries.

47

The illiterate of the 21st century will be those who cannot learn, unlearn, and relearn quickly. KM is a tool to help you learn.

48

KM captures and distributes best practices to reduce the cost of rethinking or redeveloping solutions.

49

KM provides an essential roadmap for how we connect, share, learn, and innovate. It develops relationships that make our businesses work.

50

KM allows companies to manage risk and to comply with stringent legal and compliance concerns.

51

KM reduces the loss of organizational know-how as a result of retirements and turnover.

52

KM increases revenues through real and actionable business intelligence that enables strategic decision-making.

53

KM can eliminate redundant activities and tasks. It can improve business processes and increase the speed of learning and innovating.

54

KM can foster the free flow of ideas, recognize the value of knowledge, streamline operations, and reduce the time to complete tasks.

55

KM encourages expertise more quickly so new workers become more productive, faster.

Section IV
How Do I Know My Knowledge Management
Program Is Working?

One of the most important conversations executives can have with their staff is about how they will know their KM efforts are working. Like any sound business function, you should be able to measure whether KM is having an effect on your business goals and objectives. Many people feel that KM objectives are intangible and very hard to measure. Most agree that if they can be measured, they take longer to achieve and cannot be measured on quarterly business cycles. Outlining a knowledge strategy that has clearly definable objectives and tasks is critical to a successful program. Like a roadmap, this framework helps us understand where we are going, how and when we will get there, and who is accountable for what. One of the most obvious ways you will know your KM program is working is by the behaviors that demonstrate a sense of personal accountability for continuous learning, sharing, and collaboration. People should be asking, "Who else needs to know this, who has done anything like this before, and how can we learn X so we can accomplish Y better, faster, and cheaper?"

When looking for tangible measures of effectiveness, organizations need to look at each component of the Knowledge Environment™ and identify metrics that are linked to their performance goals (i.e., growing the business base, improving profitability, increasing quality, improving brand recognition, saving time, having faster time to competency for new hires). KM should also produce a number of intangible benefits that will be much harder to measure. These benefits may include stronger relationships and networks, deeper commitment to the organization resulting in less turnover, higher sense of employee satisfaction, more collaboration, reductions in knowledge lost from retirements and transitions, and increased desire for lifelong learning...just to name a few.

56

KM is working when people naturally collaborate on new projects and take pride in sharing what they know.

57

KM is working when the demand for it to support organizationally valued operations and critical functions exceeds the KM capability.

58

KM is working when people are freely asking for help and sharing their knowledge through social connections across boundaries.

59

KM is working when new hires start producing faster as a result of a more effective onboarding program.

60

KM is working when it is no longer referred to as a program. Instead, it has become integral to organizational behavior.

61

KM is working when the KM processes improve individual, team, and organizational effectiveness.

62

KM is working when your workforce shares a common view of what is going on. They feel informed and empowered.

63

KM is working when the company lives on and communicates through the collaboration systems, not just email.

64

KM is working when employee and customer satisfaction show improvements.

Section V
Enabling and Supporting Learning in Your Organization

KM is essential to creating a learning organization. Learning is contextual, and closing the *knowledge* gaps in an organization often has a direct correlation to closing the *performance* gaps. Understanding what you *know* drives what you *do* as a company and is critical to achieving your business strategy.

KM provides valuable sources of knowledge and expertise in both formal and informal settings. Consider how you prefer to learn and whether you would prefer to learn in classrooms, in isolation, or guided by experienced and knowledgeable coaches who have performed the same types of tasks you are about to attempt. KM connects the formal and informal learning space through what we call social learning. Social learning connects people to people and people to content in more effective ways. Social learning is enabled by these connections with likeminded people with whom we can communicate and share ideas, resources, and experiences; solve business problems; and innovate and improve performance.

The Knowledge Environment™ addresses the human dynamic of learning and sense-making and goes beyond the simple acquisition of knowledge and skills. Through the connections, we are able to make sense of new constructs and build mental models to help us problem-solve more effectively. Managing the Knowledge Environment™ gives us a framework that is tangible and measurable.

KM helps us learn before, during, and after events and projects. It provides us the links to current and relevant information. It connects us with expertise and experienced people so that we can discuss, visualize, and reflect on what has been done before, how it was done, why (learning before), and what conditions are similar and different. KM allows us the means to see and share what we are doing now (learning during) with experts and rapidly compare data so that we can review and reflect on what we just did and are about to do next. KM helps us analyze the outcomes and share those lessons learned with a broader and wider range of practitioners so that others can do it better or more efficiently the next time (learning after). Effective learning organizations have deliberate approaches for learning before, during, and after in both formal and informal learning spaces. KM provides the approaches to integrate work and learning and to develop the needed "know how," as well as knowing what and why.

65

Use KM to connect people to the knowledge they need and give them the tools to create their own content to share with others.

66

Use KM activities to improve peer-to-peer interaction and support learning from each other.

67

Use KM to focus organizational energy on the human.

68

Use KM to facilitate the flow of relevant and actionable knowledge.

69

Use KM to support and enable learning by creating ways to share and access information, experiences, and insights easily and rapidly.

70

Use KM to integrate business processes and tools into a learning environment so work and classroom look very similar.

71

Use KM to see where critical knowledge and expertise reside in the organization, then connect with them.

72

KM provides the means for employees to collaborate effectively across time and geography.

73

Use KM to support user-generated content. People can create short learning modules faster than with formal methods.

74

Use KM to support social learning, an approach that combines formal and informal learning and leverages Web 2.0 technology.

75

KM is a critical component of a learning organization. Use it to develop expertise faster and share lessons learned across the company.

76

Make it a primary objective of your KM program to improve social learning by connecting the workforce in a meaningful way.

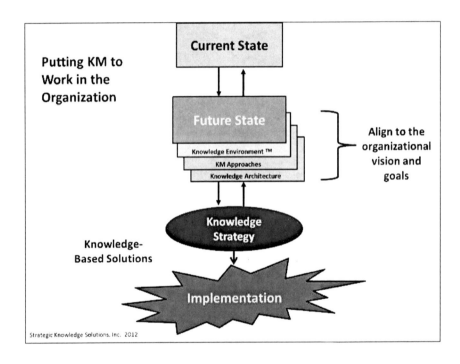

Section VI
Beginning a Knowledge Management Program in Your Organization

Starting a KM program in an organization is no small endeavor. Often the tendency is to overreach and attempt too much too fast. Sometimes we focus on areas that are the easiest to quantify and measure while ignoring the underlying behaviors we want our workforce to exhibit. Often we rely on technology to solve what are inherently human performance issues, and are thus frustrated by the lack of results. Most often we fail to communicate our KM activities in the context of work processes and desired outcomes, and neglect to link KM to solving real business problems and improving business outcomes. KM is not a one-size-fits-all approach. A good carpenter has a toolbox filled with tools designed for a specific purpose. Your approach to KM should be the same. A master carpenter knows how to employ each tool in the correct balance to achieve a desired outcome.

An effective KM program will start with an assessment, ensuring the organization's current and future state are clearly outlined and that the knowledge architecture is designed to support real business problems. KM starts with people and processes, then focuses on organizational structures, types of content needed, organizational culture, and knowledge leadership. Only then should new technology solutions be implemented. KM is about finding the relationship between a performance gap (current state) and the knowledge needed to move the organization to a desired future state. This is achieved by outlining the knowledge you will need and the behaviors that people must exhibit to close those gaps.

77

Ask yourself, "What do we want to accomplish?" instead of "How do we use X technology?"

78

Start with people first, then processes. Only then can you address KM technology to enable the activities.

79

Start your KM initiative with a knowledge assessment identifying the gaps between the current and future state.

80

Where do you start a KM program? Easy. Three key points: leadership, leadership, leadership!

81

Start your KM effort with a vision driven by business goals. Then find the right team to lead the effort.

82

Address all parts of the Knowledge Environment™: people, KM processes, technology, structure, content, culture, and knowledge leadership.

83

People are the key element of knowledge flow. Remember, systems can only move data and information. Knowledge requires relationships.

84

Develop a simple and effective change management (or change leadership) plan to guide the KM effort.

85

Identify metrics for all seven components of the Knowledge Environment™ and get the buy-in of mid- and upper-level managers early.

86

Start small. Pick a reasonable number of gaps, identify the people involved, train them on processes and tools, execute, and adjust.

87

Whether a process, form of collaboration, or use of technology, explain value in terms the customer understands and needs.

88

Reassure workers and put training in place to make them successful. Most resistance comes from those who feel their jobs are threatened.

89

When designing a KM activity, use a spiral development process.

90

Trial and error. Small wins add up. Pilot, test, adjust.

91

Your KM plan should address four phases: assess, design, develop, and implement. Anything less will result in lost time and energy.

92

Spend 60% of your time assessing so you understand the root cause of any gaps and know you are solving the right problems.

93

Sell the KM plan middle, up, down. Leaders and managers at every level must be on board. You must get buy-in from both directions.

94

Start with learning to share as a company, then practice collaborating—first in person and then virtually.

95

Include ways to push and pull knowledge and to prod users by providing reminders and alerts (like Amazon.com does with books).

96

Start with an effective communication and marketing plan that answers "What's in it for me/the workforce?"

97

Assess the organization's current KM status/practice first. Understand the organization's overall objectives.

98

Identify where the pain is. Find barriers and remove them. Look for KM-motivated people and embed them in KM development.

99

Create truly innovative solutions by solving the contradictions that most other people choose to ignore.

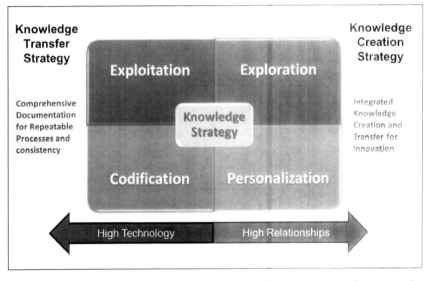

An effective knowledge strategy finds the right balance for the type of business strategy required.

Section VII
Effective Knowledge Management Strategies

Knowledge management needs to be business-led. As aforementioned, KM is not something you do for the sake of doing KM; you do it because it adds value to the business. Every KM strategy should be based on, and linked to, the business strategy. It should describe how and why the company will manage the components of the Knowledge Environment™. While there are two fundamentally different sides to KM strategies, each company will need to prioritize and choose a strategy that works best for their organization or part of their organization.

On one side of the strategy spectrum is the ability to exploit well developed procedures and perform them over and over with repeatable and consistent results. This *Knowledge Transfer Strategy* relies on codified and documented information enabled by technology to make it readily available, globally accessible, and measurable. On the other side of the spectrum is a *Knowledge Creation Strategy* that is focused on exploring new approaches, innovating, and creating new products and services. This strategy is much less dependent on technology and more reliant on personal relationships, connecting people and crossing domains to bring together ideas and solve new and complex problems. It uses KM technologies to connect people and to collaborate so as to increase the size of the team and the diversity of ideas. Every organization (or part of an organization) will have a strategy preference.

The first step is to identify the business vision and objectives, then identify the business drivers that you're going to support. The KM strategy must be short and inspiring, rather than just compelling and directive. It must communicate a vision and foster buy-in. While the framework of a KM strategy may be selected by the organizational leaders, the more participation, collaboration, and buy-in you get developing the strategy, the more chance of it getting successfully implemented.

To help with a framework, we have provided a few KM principles in Appendix A and a KM strategy template in Appendix B. How you will use these tools is directly driven by your business needs. Creating a strategy is not a difficult task, but it requires a thorough understanding of the real issues, as well as the contributing factors (not just the symptoms) and behaviors needed to close both knowledge and performance gaps. The best way to begin developing a strategy is by conducting a knowledge assessment of the organization.

100

A KM strategy begins with leadership communicating its purpose and value, and prioritizing resources to build and sustain the strategy.

101

A KM strategy must compel and inspire participation by all within the organization, and provide an action plan to guide the way forward.

102

A good KM strategy starts with a clear business use case. What, why, and how: these should drive the need for a KM program.

103

A KM strategy must include a clear link to company goals and objectives and provide a roadmap to link KM activities to business processes.

104

A KM strategy must communicate whether you are trying to maximize knowledge transfer or innovate by creating new knowledge.

105

A KM strategy should include terms of reference and definitions to help everyone speak the same language.

106

A KM strategy should include six to eight knowledge activities the organization will undertake for a successful KM program.

107

A good KM strategy includes KM processes for planning, creating, organizing, integrating, sharing, and managing the company's knowledge.

108

A strategy outlines the operating procedures that support a culture of sharing & encourages collaboration across organizational boundaries.

109

KM approaches and technology change rapidly, so the strategy must be flexible to meet the needs of the organization.

110

A good KM strategy includes a description of current and emerging technologies used by the organization and what they are used for.

111

A KM strategy provides a clear and simple map of company knowledge centers, content repositories, tools, and applications.

112

A KM strategy makes specific roles and responsibilities of the staff as they support and enable the KM program.

113

Include clear annual goals and objectives with specific tactical initiatives to be performed over the next ninety days.

114

A good KM strategy needs to be embedded in the organization's strategy with measurable, achievable, and realistic goals.

115

A KM strategy needs to bridge art and science; do not center it on technology.

116

When talking KM solutions, one size does not fit all. Every organization needs a range of approaches based on their business needs.

117

Build your strategy around enabling flow and growing expertise. Talk about how you will manage all components of the Knowledge Environment™.

118

A good KM strategy links KM practices and processes to learning in the organization.

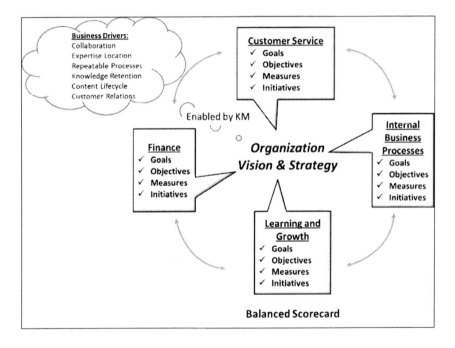

Section VIII
Advice for Creating a Sustainable Knowledge Management Program

People tend to make knowledge management much harder than it needs to be. They tend to focus on the academic arguments like the differences in data, information, and knowledge, when they should really be talking about what their organization needs to do better or differently to remain competitive and how improving knowledge flow can help achieve their goals. KM is a young discipline, and as it finds its path you should stop worrying about what it is called and orient on what it does for your organization if applied effectively.

There is no shortage of advice for what a leader starting a KM program should do first. More than 250 books and countless articles have been published in the last few years. Our contributors offer great suggestions that any leader would be well served to consider. But the most important thing an organizational leader can do is start a conversation about KM and keep it focused on supporting the business strategy. The ways and means will take care of themselves if resourced and rewarded.

We offer a few more pieces of advice to add to our contributors' good counsel: start with people, then consider the business processes you want to improve and the drivers that link KM to the business strategy. Approach KM holistically and consider each of the seven components of the Knowledge Environment™ in a balanced ecosystem that enables the flow of knowledge. And finally, keep in mind that one size does not fit all. The spectrum of KM approaches ranges from highly technical to highly relationship-driven with very little technology involved. Applying the right approach for the right gaps is the art of KM, and it takes an informed and experienced knowledge leader to execute.

119

Don't overreach and try to boil the ocean. Balance quick wins with bigger, more complex achievements to generate momentum.

120

Learn how to perform effective KM assessments, both an initial assessment and a running one.

121

Identify how knowledge gaps are related to operational gaps and then go after a KM solution.

122

A simple and effective change management (or change leadership) program will be needed to guide the KM effort.

123

Make the goals of any KM initiative clearly linked to the business processes and objectives you want to improve.

124

It is through action that knowledge adds value to an organization. Focus on making what your organization knows actionable.

125

Be specific as to what you are trying to change or learn and why.

126

Focus on knowledge flow and enabling the three types of interactions: people to people, people to content, and systems to systems.

127

Leverage technology already in use around you first; drive it to its full potential before you consider new tools and technology.

128

Find the experts in KM inside and outside the company. Leverage their experience and knowledge to build capacity in your organization.

129

Stay involved: make the achievement of KM objectives a topic at key meetings and reports. Link KM to bottom-line business improvements.

130

Build a team to implement KM across the company. Give everyone a stake in the mission and communicate what's in it for them.

131

Create value, not just activity. Focus on what is organizationally meaningful and important; time and resources are valuable.

132

When getting started on a KM initiative, develop a phased approach and set realistic goals.

133

Don't talk about what KM can do until you have assessed the organization and its leadership.

134

Establish a vision of the "possible" in doing old things in a new way and become a master of the fundamentals of change management.

135

A good knowledge leader not only provides opportunities, but encourages and rewards management at all levels to share what they know.

136

KM needs dedicated oversight just like HR, IT, budgeting, etc. Find a KM lead with an operational perspective.

137

Focus on human interactions
more than technology.
Technology must enable the
people-to-people interactions.

138

Do not assume that your
preconceived notions of what ails an
organization are in fact correct.

139

A good knowledge leader is one who excels at and enables the understanding of the role of knowledge development and sharing in the company.

140

KM is part art and part science. The art deals with intangibles, as does leadership. Get comfortable talking about the intangibles.

What Are Your Ahas?

Thank you for reading *#SUCCESSFUL CORPORATE LEARNING tweet Book05*!
Got any "ahas" that would fit with this book?
We'd love to read them! Please send us your ahas
by visiting the following URL:

http://tinyurl.com/whatareyourahas

Appendix A: Sample Knowledge Management Principles

These KM principles provide some commonly accepted rules of action observed in many of the companies we have worked with over the past six years. We don't suggest that you adopt all twelve principles, but rather, select three to six key principles that resonate with your business and the priorities driven by your company strategy. Use the principles to start and focus conversations about KM and guide the development of your KM strategy. These principles provide priorities in a KM strategy and help you focus the resources and approaches you will apply to the KM program.

KM Principles

FLOW: Knowledge must move to be useful. It must flow in a deliberate and disciplined way through an organization. Knowledge increases in value as it is used. As such, organizations should focus on developing and implementing a knowledge strategy that manages the components of the Knowledge Environment™ and ensures the flow of knowledge from people to people, people to information, and systems to systems.

SHARE: Knowledge is a transferable asset that tends to grow with use and application. Designing, promoting, and sustaining an organizational culture that shares effectively is the first step in developing a learning organization. Knowledge only moves through people. The new mantra should be "Knowledge Shared Is Power."

CONNECT: Connecting people is a prerequisite to the creation of an effective learning organization. It is through connection that knowledge is not only shared but created. Knowledge creation depends on knowledge transfer from those with experience, expertise, and insight to those who need to develop the knowledge, skills, and perspectives to work at higher levels of performance. This requires connecting people to people and people to the right knowledge sources. Organizations must identify and eliminate barriers to connecting. Create virtual water coolers and global hallways where people can connect and share effortlessly.

COLLABORATE: Collaboration—where individuals work together to create something greater than that which is created alone—is the key to process improvement. Collaboration must be enabled for both local and virtual teams to succeed. Collaboration must occur across time and across geographical and cultural boundaries. Do not leave collaboration to happenstance; have deliberate processes in place to ensure effective work across all boundaries. Dedicate a part of every meeting to collaboration.

CULTIVATE: We cultivate knowledge when we add to, comment on, and debate, discuss, or improve content created by others. By cultivating conversation, we learn from one another, improve relationships, and feel better about where we work and who we work with. Cultivating a culture of sharing and collaboration also involves rewards and recognition for the positive behaviors expected.

TRUST: Successful KM depends on the willingness to share knowledge so that others can benefit, and to reach outside the boundaries of hierarchical structures to cultivate relationships and connections. This sharing provides the foundation for building an environment of trust and mutual understanding and demands a certain level of control be placed in the hands of employees. Give trust before demanding trustworthiness.

PREVENT KNOWLEDGE LOSS: Effective organizations identify and capture the knowledge, expertise, and wisdom of experienced workers before they leave the company. Effective *learning* organizations create a deliberate approach to share that knowledge to improve learning and performance.

ACCESS: Make knowledge accessible while still protecting intellectual property and trade secrets. Core knowledge must be visible to all. Systems must be user-friendly and facilitate both knowledge and expertise location.

PROTECT AND SECURE: Governance, risk management, and compliance requirements dictate how we must protect and secure our corporate information and knowledge assets. Share as much as possible while establishing sound accountability procedures. Make breaching organizational trust unacceptable rather than preventing access to needed information and knowledge resources.

USE COMMON, INTUITIVE TOOLS: In today's knowledge environment, one size does not fit all. Tools must be customized to the organization and its collaborative needs, yet intuitive and ubiquitous. Use commercial off-the-shelf tools and applications wherever possible. Eliminate "not invented here" attitudes regarding tools on the part of both information technology and executive staffs. Think mobile. Allow users to work from anywhere, at any time, on any device, as far as organizational policy will allow.

GET ORGANIZED: Content comes in many forms that must be managed differently. Effective content management must include managing both expertise (tacit knowledge) and documentation (explicit knowledge) for the benefit of the organization. Use robust search tools. Keep document repositories organized and flat. Encourage professional networking and expertise locations by ensuring employee profiles are complete and up to date. Map all systems, processes, repositories, and technology tools for everyone to see. Train new workers during onboarding as well as periodically to inculcate and refresh the organization's knowledge culture.

LEAD: The impact of KM on an organization is directly proportional to the level of leadership and management involvement. While much of KM offers intangible results, many concrete benefits can be measured in terms of organizational objectives. Behavior, trust, and incentives affect organizational learning and performance. Used together, these elements will set conditions for a culture of learning and sharing in the organization. Good knowledge leaders need not use every tool, but they should ensure useful tools are available to knowledge workers, access is easy, people are trained, and knowledge is cultivated, captured, and disseminated to the organization.

Appendix B: Knowledge Management Strategy Development Outline

1. **PURPOSE & STRATEGY**
   The first part of the strategy provides the foundation for KM in the organization and specifically explains why the company needs KM and how it will be used. It links KM to company goals and objectives, and addresses business drivers that KM supports by answering the fundamental KM question: "What must we be able to do?" (i.e., the actual behavior that must be performed). Determine the strategy to improve knowledge flow, collaboration, and sharing to achieve that business objective.

   This section also includes a brief explanation of what type of knowledge is most important to the organization (tacit or explicit), and how organizational processes and tools support the strategy. This can most easily be expressed by aligning the organization's knowledge strategy along a continuum. At one end of the continuum is a strategy that focuses on connecting people to create new knowledge, learn faster, and develop expertise. At the other end is a strategy that focuses on connecting people with information or content so they can perform repeatable processes and deliberate procedures the same way every time.

   This section may also outline regulatory guidelines that the organization must follow regarding information and knowledge management. These requirements should not be primary business drivers but must be made known to the organization. Specifics and references may be included in a periodically updated annex.

2. **KM VISION & MISSION**

    This section outlines the leadership vision for KM in the organization and defines a mission statement tying KM to organizational goals. These statements explain how KM can be used to flatten the organization, improve collaboration, and synchronize knowledge across all elements of the organization in pursuit of business objectives.

3. **KM GOALS & OBJECTIVES**

    KM goals and objectives are the focus of the strategy. This section outlines three to four specific goals (each with three to five measurable objectives) for the KM program over the period of time addressed by the strategy. These goals and objectives tie directly to the business drivers identified in Section 1 and move the organization along the path toward achieving its KM vision. These goals and objectives are not short-term tasks, which are addressed later in the strategy. Rather, these goals and objectives explain what the organization must do to achieve success in the KM program and how that success will be measured.

4. **KM PRINCIPLES**

    Much of KM is common sense, and common core principles provide guidelines for success. This section contains organization-specific principles that convey the priorities and intent of leadership with respect to KM. Part philosophy and part behavior norms, these principles guide the organization as it implements a knowledge-based culture. See Appendix A for examples of commonly used KM principles.

5. **THE KNOWLEDGE ENVIRONMENT™**

    This section outlines the components of the Knowledge Environment™ and how the organization will manage these components to support the business drivers affecting organizational performance. It establishes and helps communicate the tangible ways, means, and ends that KM will facilitate accomplishing the business objectives.

    Specifically, this section addresses the organization's view and definitions of:

- KM processes
- People
- Technology
- Organizational structure
- Content
- Organizational culture
- Knowledge leadership

6. **TERMS OF REFERENCE**
This section establishes a shared understanding and a common KM vocabulary for the organization. It should address the top ten to fifteen terms required for understanding and applying the organization's KM strategy. These terms should be used frequently when talking about sharing knowledge so they become part of the language of the company. Many companies define terms in a strategy annex where they can be easily overlooked. Embedding them in the body of the strategy and providing organizational rationales along with definitions puts the terms in context. This context supports shared understanding, a key element of culture change.

7. **ORGANIZATIONAL ROLES AND RESPONSIBILITIES**
This section outlines the specific roles and responsibilities of the staff, business units, and employees as they enable, implement, and support the KM program. These roles and responsibilities should be expressed in an organizational sense to identify champions and leaders responsible for aligning KM goals and objectives and implementing KM initiatives with respect to business drivers.

8. **KM APPROACHES**
This section outlines the four basic approaches to KM solutions discussed in Section VI of this book.

- Self-service
- Process-based KM
- Network-based KM
- Expertise development & continuous learning

Specifically, this section develops the understanding that not all KM is about document management and relates when the four different approaches are most useful to the company. The approaches range from high technology/high codification approaches that connect people to information to high relationship/personalization approaches that connect people to people to share expertise. This section creates the foundation for how the company will implement a full range of knowledge services and outlines the priorities based on the knowledge strategy expressed in Sections 1-3 of this outline.

9. **MAKING KNOWLEDGE VISIBLE**
This section identifies (by list or maps in a graphic representation) where crucial knowledge required to perform work and achieve the organization's business strategy is located. It also identifies current and emerging technologies and tools used to assist in the management of that knowledge. It must describe what each tool/technology is used for, and how it relates to organizational business processes.

10. **ACTION PLAN**
This section outlines KM strategy implementation. It describes "how" you will implement the strategy and is reported upon regularly and updated quarterly. It defines how the organization will achieve its goals and objectives. It consists of two parts: initiatives and general operating procedures.

10.1. **KM INITIATIVES**
This section outlines the immediate tasks that must be performed in the next three to six months and establishes accountability and milestones for each. Each task links directly to a KM goal and objective (from Section III) and a business driver (from Section I). This section should be reported upon regularly (typically monthly) and updated on a recurring basis (typically quarterly) as goals and objectives are achieved.

For some KM strategies, a longer time horizon is required to support the organization's overall planning cycle. If this is the case, then short-term, mid-term, and long-term tasks should be identified. The following table provides a helpful framework.

Business Driver:				
KM Goal:		KM Objective:		
Priority Tasks	Expected Outcomes	Mapping to Organization's Core Processes	Responsible Party	Date Due

10.2. **KM GENERAL OPERATING PROCEDURES**
This section outlines the operating procedures that support a culture of collaboration and encourage sharing across organizational boundaries. It also provides the guidelines and intent for collaborative activities like creating and developing cross-disciplinary teams, on-boarding and off-boarding employees, conducting meetings, email use, briefings, reports, etc.

Leadership Signatures and Coordinating Lines

It is important to show support from the organization's leadership and buy-in from each department and level of the organization. The true test of a Strategy Document is what people do, not what's written on paper.

Appendix: Bibliographies and References

In this section, list the references that support your KM strategy and bibliographies that provide the academic and foundational thinking for the strategy.

Appendix C: References

Baxter, Holly, and Michael Prevou. "A Method for Effectively Assessing Knowledge in Organizations." Presented at the *International Conference on Knowledge Management. Proceedings of the International Conference on Knowledge Management*. Pittsburgh, PA: 2010.

Drucker, Peter F. *The New Realities: In Government and Politics, in Economics and Business, in Society and World View*. New York: Harper & Row, 1989.

Economist Intelligence Unit. "Foresight 2020: Economic, Industry and Corporate Trends." *The Economist*. 2006. http://graphics.eiu.com/files/ad_pdfs/eiuForesight2020_WP.pdf.

O'Dell, Carla, and Cindy Hubert. *The New Edge in Knowledge: How Knowledge Management Is Changing the Way We Do Business*. New Jersey: Wiley, 2011.

Prevou, Michael. "Understanding the Knowledge Environment." *Army Communicator* 36, no. 2 (2011): 49-53. http://bit.ly/Pfhtjl.[1]

Sveiby, Karl-Erik. "Knowledge Management – Lessons from the Pioneers." 2001. http://bit.ly/omoLxD.[2]

---

1. www.signal.army.mil/ArmyCommunicator/2011/Vol36/No2/ 2011Vol36No2Sub17.pdf

2. www.providersedge.com/docs/km_articles/KM_-_Lessons_from_ the_Pioneers.pdf

About the Authors

Michael (Mike) Prevou, PhD, is president and co-founder of Strategic Knowledge Solutions, a leading consulting firm specialized in knowledge management (KM) and organizational learning solutions.

Mike is one of the most innovative and experienced KM practitioners in the country. He is a certified Master Knowledge Management Professional and in *#SUCCESSFUL CORPORATE LEARNING tweet Book05: Everything You Need to Know about Knowledge Management in Practice in 140 Characters or Less*, he draws on that unique experience in the public, private, and non-profit sectors to bring you the most relevant and cutting-edge developments in the field.

Mike spent twenty-five years in the U.S. Army, where he co-founded the Army's lead agency on knowledge management and established and grew a nested network of over sixty online communities of practice to connect Army leaders. These communities have now grown to over 250,000 active members and have saved the military time, money, and lives. He has consulted with over thirty corporate, military, federal government, and academic organizations on KM and learning and published over twenty-five articles on knowledge management strategies and solutions, and individual, team, and organizational learning approaches. He is a regular speaker at learning and knowledge management conferences and teaches a series of KM related courses, workshops, and seminars. His unique experiences in implementing real KM in action along with his background in educational psychology partner for a powerful combination of expertise that can help any company implement a successful KM program targeted to their specific needs.

Mitchell Levy is the author of twelve business books and the CEO of the independent publishing house Happy About®. After earning his MBA from the College of William and Mary, he spent thirteen years working for corporations in IT, Finance, and Operations. He then spent eleven years as an entrepreneur creating thirteen companies and strategic partnerships, including Happy About in 2005. During this timeframe, he created over seventy courses at various universities and online learning programs, and booked over 500 speakers at large-scale conferences.

Mr. Levy is also partner of the physical networking firm CXOnetworking and sits on the Board of Directors at Rainmaker Systems (NASDAQ: RMKR). Previously, he created four executive education programs at two different Silicon Valley universities and was the conference chair for four Comdex conferences focusing on business executives at medium to large sized enterprises. He has contributed to and written over 100 articles, and has given over 250 speeches on e-commerce and business.

Books in the THiNKaha® Series

The THiNKaha book series is for thinking adults who lack the time or desire to read long books, but want to improve themselves with knowledge of the most up-to-date subjects. THiNKaha is a leader in timely, cutting-edge books and mobile applications from relevant experts that provide valuable information in a fun, Twitter-brief format for a fast-paced world.

They are available online at http://thinkaha.com or at other online and physical bookstores.

1. *#BOOK TITLE tweet* by Roger C. Parker
2. *#BUSINESS SAVVY PM tweet* by Cinda Voegtli
3. *#COACHING tweet* by Sterling Lanier
4. *#CONTENT MARKETING tweet* by Ambal Balakrishnan
5. *#CORPORATE CULTURE tweet* by S. Chris Edmonds
6. *#CORPORATE GOVERNANCE tweet* by Brad Beckstead, CPA, CISA, CRISC
7. *#CROWDSOURCING tweet* by Kiruba Shankar and Mitchell Levy
8. *#CULTURAL TRANSFORMATION tweet* by Melissa Lamson
9. *#DEATHtweet Book01: A Well-Lived Life through 140 Perspectives on Death and Its Teachings* by Timothy Tosta
10. *#DEATH tweet Book02: 140 Perspectives on Being a Supportive Witness to the End of Life* by Timothy Tosta
11. *#DIVERSITYtweet* by Deepika Bajaj
12. *#DOG tweet* by Timothy Tosta and Nancy Martin
13. *#DREAMtweet* by Joe Heuer
14. *#ENDURANCE tweet* by Jarie Bolander
15. *#ENTRYLEVELtweet Book01: Taking Your Career from Classroom to Cubicle* by Heather R. Huhman
16. *#ENTRY LEVEL tweet Book02: Relevant Advice for Students and New Graduates in the Day of Social Media* by Christine Ruff and Lori Ruff
17. *#EXPERT EXCEL PROJECTS tweet* by Larry Moseley
18. *#GOOGLE+ for BUSINESS tweet* by Janet Fouts
19. *#HEALTHCARE REFORM tweet* by Jason T. Andrew

THiNKaha® Learning/Training Programs Designed to Take You to the Next Level NOW!

THiNKaha® delivers high-quality, cost-effective continuous learning in easy-to-understand, worthwhile, and digestible chunks. Fifteen minutes with a THiNKaha® book will allow readers to have one or more "aha" moments. Spending less than two hours a month with a THiNKaha® Learning Program (either online or in person) will provide learners with an opportunity to truly digest the topic at hand and connect with gurus whose subject-matter expertise gives them an actionable roadmap to enhance their skills.

Offered online, on demand, and/or in person, these engaging programs feature gurus (ours and yours) on such relevant topics as Leadership, Management, Sales, Marketing, Work-Life Balance, Project Management, Social Media and Networking, Presentation Skills, and other topics of your choosing. The "learning" audience, whether it is clients, employees, or partners, can now experience high-quality learning that will enhance your brand value and empower your company as a thought leader. This program fits a real need where time and the high cost of developing custom content are no longer an option for every organization.

"This program has been very successful and in demand within Cisco. The vision and implementation of the THiNKaha Learning Program has enabled us to offer high-quality content both live and on-demand. Their gurus and experts are knowledgeable and very engaging."

- Bette Daoust, Ph.D
Former Learning and Development Manager, Cisco, and Internal Program Manager for THiNKaha Guru Series

Visit THiNKaha® Learning Program at http://thinkaha.com/learning.

Just **THiNK**...

- **C**ontinuous Employee/Client/Prospect Learning
- **O**ngoing Thought Leadership Development
- **N**otable Experts Presenting on Relevant Topics
- **T**ime Your Attendees Can Afford – 15 min. to 2 hrs/mo.
- **I**nformation Delivered in Digestible Chunks
- **N**ame the Topic—We Help You Provide Expert Best Practices
- **U**nderstand and Implement the Takeaways
- **I**nternal Expertise Shared Externally
- **T**raining/Prospecting Cost Decreases, Effectiveness Increases
- **Y**ou Win, They Win!

CPSIA information can be obtained at www.ICGtesting.com
Printed in the USA
LVOW131121300812

296634LV00001BA/1/P